Launch Out Into the Deep
Deep Calls to the Deep

by

E. A. Simmons

DORRANCE
PUBLISHING CO
EST. 1920
PITTSBURGH, PENNSYLVANIA 15222

Dorrance Publishing Co.
701 Smithfield Street
Pittsburgh, PA 15222
Visit our website at *www.dorrancebookstore.com*

ISBN: 978-1-4349-3720-9
eISBN: 978-1-4349-3640-0

Forbidden Love

A change in my life has got to be in me.
I can't keep this lifestyle up, I know that it's killing me.
This is one thing that I know from the first moment she
and I met. We have been having this torrent love affair and it's
not over yet.
I want to let her go but she love my money.
Broke before the night falls now I feel funny.
Any money that I get I give to this my whore.
She follows me everywhere even to the church and the liquor store.
Then the bitch get jazzy and leaves me alone but because I can't
get any more…
Then payday comes, and I run, but it's not into the arms
of my wife, see' she don't understand.
But it's into the arms of my forbidden lover,
one toke and I am free, free to kill myself feeling sorry
about my past drug history.
taking aim at the target that's in front of me, my
future. No brass no ammo drill sergeant, and no alibis anymore..
Life doesn't suck, I do. So-called friends will not stay away from
my front door.
Temptation is a wolf in sheep's clothing, who knows that you
are trying to quit. But he/she has ammo and they don't want
you to quit.
This is the bottom the 9th it's your time at bat.
Don't worry about anyone else it's your ball and bat.

Walking Dead

People are always talking about, Man, I wish that I could
see a ghost. Well, I just saw three walk by, the reason that
I say that is that you don't have to give up the ghost to
die. You can be a dead man walking, and not somewhere lying
in a lonesome grave. Mr Ridle Mr Hagler and Mr. Palmer are
gone in the blink of an eye, like a puff of smoke a dream
One solemn wave. The quick and the dead, not either or. there
is no in between. If you want to see a ghost you don't have to
wait, till Halloween.

My Eyes

My eye sight is pitiful, it once was 20/20.
Now I can't even see myself. Other people see me plainly
even if they are blind. Hindsight 20/20 not yours I'm
talking about mine…Weigh in the balance of life I hope
that I'm not found wanting. Life and death of the two
life is what I'm wanting.
My health, I feel like a sack of shit, I might need to borrow
a turd. A flash of lighting before my eyes. God's voice I
have never heard. I have told people about the thing that
I have seen, they look at me as if I'm crazy. I don't have
to ask you to make water, kiss my ass, Miss Daisy.
That don't help my physical being none like a couple of
sit-up and pull-up would do. I almost get a nosebleed trying
to tie my shoe.

Lucky Boy

If I was your daddy I would whip your little ass,
acting like you can't get right.
The next time that I would bring him out with me he would
be forty-five years old & and it would be at midnight.
Maybe it's because I was raised in the country,
you know the country way.
And if you knew my father and mother, you know that they
did not play.
If you heard behave (bay heave) that means that your butt
was in danger.
Not only from getting an ass whipping from aunts and uncles
Sometimes even from total strangers
So you are a lucky child very lucky indeed
Because coming up with us you would have gotten your ass whipped
until you peed.

E/Z

What about me, I want to be free. Free and clean and not be mean.
No dope in my temple, thinking clean and make life simple.
E/Z does it one day at a time. I control my life I take back mine
So E/Z does it just for today and please have mercy on me this I pray.

Gone but Not Forgotten

Never never land is where my (M F S B) now dwell,
(M mother F father S sister B brother)
Longing to see their essence the, very spirit of love.
Life on earth is a test that we either pass or fail.
JESUS came and was baptized by John in the River Jordan.
The sign that he was the one was a dove.
JESUS and his father talks to my family, speaking of days gone by.
The times of trials and tribulations. The times that they had to cry,
AS Tim raps with JESUS he looks as his crown filled with
diamonds and says, "What are these, my Lord."
He replies, "Remember when things got bad and people didn't
understand. And you wept as I did?"
He says, "Yes, my Lord.
Each tear I saved in a bottle, now they are diamonds in
your crown that you wear for eternity, my friend.
See, it all will pay off in the end."
My mother did the same way; she stayed with my father until the end.
She tells GOD and JESUS, "I'm going to make you a quilt,"
like the ones she made with love in every stitch.
JESUS tells Mom to do "what you want because I know that
guilt will come from your heart.
You raised the ten gifts I gave you, well, they are the
diamonds in your crown.
And, George, thank you for the blackberries and plums you
gave me; yes, your life was harder than most, because you have
loved when you really didn't know what love was.
But your family stayed together, brother, now that was very hard."
They all even Kattie has something for JESUS, you know,
Kattie she is going to give JESUS some fish that has that
little twing to them, and a rabbit and some other stuff
that he will say thank you for.
Your diamonds are your kids and grandkids. You bleed
for them as I did up there on that cross for the family

that you loved. Kattie, please rest awhile, but Kattie won't
you know her, she's all over heaven, walking around talking
to everyone she meets.
And she wants to make sure that that is real gold out
there on the streets
Now they cast down their crowns at JESUS' feet and
declared, "Worthy is the lamb that died for us all."
WE pray for the rest of our family and friends
to make it in before its everlasting too late y'all.

Anyway Pray

Why am I praying? Is it for real?
Or is it to appease God and the way it makes me feel?
Cheated on my wife, send up a prayer.
Had sex with a minor, pray or risk the dare.
To play with hellfire, I stole a car.
The Ten Commandments are not for me they take life too far.
Man, you have a beautiful wife and family, they are one of a kind.
I pray and wish that I had them for myself,
I want to make them mine.

My Nigger

I did it again, my brother, I forgot that I was black.
Like the white man I looked at that nigger and I cut him no slack.
He was black and stinky. I don't care if he had just gotten off
work. My nose went up in the air. Damn now I feel like
a fucking jerk. I would change my clothes every evening, and
put on my favorite cologne. Thinking that I was better than
that brother, man I was wrong. Nobody gave a damn about
how clean I was, the oldspice made me stink.
See, as long as you are black and you're asshole points toward
the ground you are a nigger. That's the way the white man thinks.

Why Not?

Why was I not made of stone like these? Not only me but the
whole world. Not to have joined into this cosmic swirl.
Heart have turned to stone. Love as hard as a rock.
But not the rock of ages. The only place that you can
find love now a day are in the Bible pages.
Well, they have been taken over by the computer and the Internet
I have visited some of those sites and some I'd like to forget.
Then my eyes turn to stone. The time that I spun with my
Wife dwindles till there is none. Up all night till the
rising of the sun. It's scary to me that anything that
you want to see will pop up on my computer screen.
I have seen shit over in the middle of the night.
I'm talking about stuff that I never seen and don't know.
If I'll ever be right

Here He Comes

Here he comes, y'all, the lover of my soul. Here he comes
Y'all the protector of us all.
The one that made the dead man walk,
The one that beat all night long,
The one that made the dumb tongue to talk.
The crucified one without any broken bones.
The lion of the tribe of Judea
without beginning with an end.
The king of kings the ruler of rulers
The one that sticks closer than a brother
The one that spoke to the wind and sea.
The one that was told about by my mother.
The one that die for you and me.

Me, Myself, and I

Who is that that Say yes when I try to say no. Doing wrong
instead of right, He keep me up until the wee hours of
the morning Firing a shot without any warning. Going places
where I don't belong, singing the word without the music
to the song, Thinking about how I can get into someone's
pocket. Dammit, negro, please try and stop it. if I could
have I would have a long time ago myself. I see some people
do it all by themselves. Damn the torpedoes full speed ahead
Or at least until (you!) our mission is dead. We've been doing
Our master's bidding on you since the beginning of your
time. And we got close to you when we took your wife's mine.
Damn we missed so we reload again. This time we will get
you by using your so-called friend.
No you won't because I can see clearly now that the fog
is gone, I can see all obstacles in my way. Gone are the
dark clouds that had me blind. It's going to be a bright
sunshiny day..

This pit stop at the VA is to check under the hood of this '55 model
I've been driving.
The VA has been
flagging me in for three years now and I am just now arriving
coming in for a landing, even if I have to crash and burn.
Some things in life are free; well, it took me a long time to learn.
Oh, well, crash if I have to burn if I must, I'll see what
Comes out with the settling of the dust. A lot
of vets have made it and I know that I can do the same,
We tried to pass the buck, but no we now accept the
blame. As the Phoenix Bird does we all will rise from the ashes
This was one hell of a test to the brotherhood of recovering
Vets to the right of passages.

KJV

I did pretty good without modern man, my word stood the test
of time,
And then along came willie Joe neckbone who knows Me
better than I do myself. Well, he must be a reader of minds,
He put his words where mine used to be, he
did write his own Bible. I guess. Because what you all read
in today's churches ain't nothing but a pure mess.
My voice is no longer in my word, mere man stole
them and hid them away.
The words you read now no longer contain my love for you,
so it's for you I pray.
Was not the KJV good enough? No you had to revise it time
and time again.
Now when you finish reviving it, no one will ever know if
there were ever any thing know as sin.
I said my way are not your ways and higher are my thoughts
than yours. When people read the KJV, it's like something
they never heard.

Our Father

I met the Father of all this morning, I met the great I Am today. I met him in a simple form as I started my morning, kneeling down to pray. I used to be afraid to try to talk to him, I guess that I didn't know any better. Then he told me why I was that way; he said it was the trick of the devil. "Don't you see that I love you, and I will never do you no harm. The enemy has lied to you and made you afraid. He hates you, don't be alarmed. See, I am with you always from the time that you are born until you die. I have set up with you at night and comforted you when you cried. The job, your wife, family, and friends I gave them all to you. I knew that you would find me in time; all you needed was the truth. I won't make you act like a fool, like the devil had you thinking. He tried to kill you and your family and a lot of others when you were driving and drinking. Now that you have found me, tell your friends that you have been born again, and that they can do the same. See, I am getting ready to destroy this wicked world of sin."

If I could void my mistake, my life would be not mine. I need help from God today please.

Day Off

On a cold and heartless night, when the grim reaper took a vacation, all over the world people were not dying from disease over dose or starvation. The drive-by didn't happen, and the child that cried didn't get slammed against the wall. The man that lost everything that he had said, "I'm not going to jump at all. The robber and the murderer stopped to have a drink at their favorite bar. They didn't go out to do their job of blowing up that unfaithful spouse's car. Itchy and Scratchy they even chilled out, yes, Itchy laid down his knife." Then everyone on earth remembered the story, Of it's a wonderful life. One of these days, this life will be gone, and life as we know it will be no more. When death goes back on the job, will he come knocking at your door? I love life and I love death. After death, we would just begin to live. Eternity is a very long time, but from God, to you he freely gives.

Your Day

I woke up on the wrong side of the road today,
as the day just begun.
I had time to change it so I did before the rising of the sun.
I wanted my day to start off right,
I had to forget what I did last night.
cranking it up early, starting off where I left of at some where
around four.
Did not get much sleep three hours later my day began as I
open my front door.
I believe that a man that has no addition is a man with
very little pain.
And a man that has an addition is a man that will never
come in out of the rain.

Every Ain't

Every ghost ain't holy, every shut eye is not asleep.
A man is known by the company he keeps.

Just Do It

Pick your move, choose your path, the one that you will
travel every day, Do you go left or do you go right?
Do you let it go or do you fight?
Do you go up or do you go around?
Do you go through the country
or do you go through town?
Do you cut bait or fish?
Do you go get it, or make a wish?
Do we sit down or do we stand up?
Do we pray to GOD to take this bitter cup?
Am I one in a million that are lost, now I know that GOD
has given me a cross?
Do I look on as the world goes on to hell?
Or do I sound the alarm and sound the church bell?
So pick and chose all you got is your soul to lose
So good night and may GOD bless,
and to all the other Soldiers
I say PARADE REST …

See/Saw

You did't see what I saw, so you can't say what I see.
I saw a shooting star, and little ducks like submarines.
I saw the most beautiful girl in my world, I saw her in my
dream. Do you dream of monster and such? Do you take day
trips in your mind? What are these trailers that I see? Are they
from too much food or to much fortified wine. Most of them
are nice; I have only had three or four that had me looking
under my bed. The kind that I love the most are the ones when
I wake up
I have a boner between my legs. Sometimes I don't know her
Ten times out of nine I do, so let me have my time with her
at night pretty please and thank you.

Too Much Is Too Much

The food is good everyone's getting fat.
The reason why is that are not drinking and smoking crack.
Every day at the same time the chow comes to us.
If I don't watch myself I will surely bust.
But some can't seem to get that old man out of their system.
If they did the drugs the way they eat, the food would kill
them. Now we feel rich because we eat pizza and Kentucky
Fired Chicken. That don't impress me at all, now stop that bitchin'.

Preaching to the Church

Back to basic training to retrain my mind, body, & soul
Listen to the wind for a sign of change before I get too old.
See my body squeaks like a mouse running through the church
at night. I want to stop doing what I do jang-a-lang jang-a-lang
cannot get right. I used to kick a helicopter out of the sky,
cannot do that anymore. Now, I'm trying to kick the trash
to the curb that keeps walking up to my door. The Devil
that travels in the circles that I do, it has thirty-five days
to practice its art of deception to get me back in the game.
If I go back to doing the way that I was, I have only myself to blame.
Aces and eights, the dead man's hand, so bow out now
and be free. I'm talking to everyone in this programs
to myself, yes, especially to me...

The Talk of the Rock Cry Out

The valley of the sycamore tree were the dead men dwell.
Their tombstones tell their story; the headstone does its
job well. Who they were, where they came from? A little bit
of a heroes' life. On the backside of some is written the name
of their loving wife. Today is Thanksgiving Day, the year
2012. The rain might run me back to my room. Looks like
it has settled in, yes, the rain looks like it has its bags
with it, looks like it's here to stay.
To cut off some of my writing outside on this Thanksgiving Day.

Jesus Is Love

Now I know what love is about, it's more than just a feeling. It's more than a house or home, four walls and a ceiling. Love runs deep, my friend, deeper than any sea or ocean. Love is not a feeling, and it's not some kind of emotion. Love is from your heart and spirit. For love you don't have to beg. Love is true, and it comes from God, and it's not between your mate's legs. Love is freely given, and you don't have to ask for it. Love is still loving someone when you thirst, and they give you vinegar on a stick Love is letting no power on earth keep you after being three days in the ground. Love is putting up with all that, just to get to wear your crown. Love is love, that is all I can say, and love will always please us. Love is yours and love is mine. There's no greater love than Jesus.

Old Prayer

What I think I'll do is drink and smoke until I die.
Or at least until Jesus splits the eastern sky.
Please give me a second chance, brother, I'll be okay.
I am living off the prayer of my mom & pop when for me
they would pray.
I don't know what they said to GOD, and I'll probably never
know. Or find out. All I know is I would repeat those words
for a better tomorrow for me without a doubt.
Is it the words or the person from which the words come
that make the lame walk and let you hear the voice of the
dumb?

At the Door

The witch is at my door, wanting to see if I want to come out and play.

I say, "Thanks for the concern. You can now be on your merry way." When the bell tolls the hour of the witch, beware, my junky friend. The next time you might not hear it because you got caught up in your sin.

Dumb Boy

How bad can it get? This is not a dream it is for real
Ain't no need of crying over the past. start, reach into
the future, and make something that is going to last.
Don't go back to the thing that took your joy,
If I do, I am a very dumb boy.

Lock Up

I was not there when they put him in the ground.
Instead my black ass was locked up downtown.
I was not there when they thought dirt in his face.
Instead I was locked up in my cell in this jailhouse place.

Change

I have seen the hood change; now, on the other hand, It seems
to be no way for me to do the same
I want to change for better, and I try day by day,
Now the backhoes they hoe, and the dozer they doze.
Down goes one, bam, up comes three in its place.
Change should be so easy in
my life. But I'm on the inside looking out, it's a disgrace.
A makeover is what I need, no re-zone, re-district, rehab,
or just remodel. I'll be kicking one down if I can get
rid of the crack and those 40oz bottles.

Just Because

Well, I can see downtown, but that don't mean that I'm going.
My nose is running, but my nose I might not be blowing.
Just because I washed my ass, don't mean that it won't be stanking
I bought that 40,oz and that don't mean I'll be dranking.
If I go to church for forty years, then go straight to hell what
does that mean?
If I sit up there with the choir, do I have to sing?
The ups and downs
The things I did or the things
that I didn't.
So let it be done,
well, so let it be
written.

He's By My Side

Things just don't feel the same out here, walking by myself
I felted much better with my buddy, instead of walking by myself
Everything had to move and get out of the way, but not now
because I am walking by myself.
I haven't ventured out in days, I got to get used to walking by myself.
But I have him in spirit and GOD, so I am not walking by
myself. The spirit will never leave you, so I am never alone,
or walking by myself...

The Help

If I stop this program, who do I hurt? ME.
I just opened my blind eyes so that I might see.
The things on the outside, I see the ones that will do me harm.
But then the inside me welcomes death with open arms.
A bag of dope, a bottle of beer, what do you think I am doing here?
Fighting the yen side daily seems like the yan never wins
This might be for me my last recovery; I am going to take
it on the chin.
"It's all about a change," I once heard a wise man say,
"You can't do a thing about tomorrow and not a thing about
yesterday."

From the Inside Out

In the enemy camp, looking out from the stand point of war.
I would hire the best of the best to kill my enemy and keep score.
If he likes killing time, then I would give him someone
to keep blank his mind.
If he like smoking dope and that was his choice,
I'd send someone with a lot of money, different
people of course

I at a time I would send them by, getting him weaker and weaker
He very soon will die.
I would surround him with spirit killer. Some
family, others, old friends; see, it's the little foxes
that destroy the vine. He better come to his senses quick
because he is running out of time.
Now I know what Tim was talking about. When he said,
"If you want to live you'd better move."
As for me and my house, the side of the Lord I have to choose.

Got Ya

I walk down the road alone drugs have kept me away from people that I love. I say, "Get behind me, Satan," but seems, like he always shoves. I am so tired of doing wrong I know that the devil just sits back and grin. He probably says to his demons, "See, I got old Ernest again." Now I want to make my God happy with the things that my life brings forth. To give my testimony to this world, and to make this life living well worth.

Good Deed

Well, I have done my good deed for this week.
I just got through feeding a bunch of niggers.
Those greedy bastards; every day the lines get longer and bigger
If you say free food, especially fried chicken.
Here they come skinning ginning finger popping bullshitting.

The Angel

An angel spoke to me the other day the only thing is it was one
That he had fell from heaven,
The other thing is that he started a long time ago when
I was ten or eleven.
Look, you would be better off not walking but running.
Standing not sitting making it happen and not just wishing.

Hallelujah

The rocks sang hallelujah as the water flowed right on by.
The birds shout praises the God of creation, from up on high
The earth saying hallelujah as the sun came through the clouds,
I sang hallelujah, because I know Jesus, and for that I am proud.

The Rest of My God

The rest of my God is the rest that we all need. Just follow Jesus today, don't you know and have you not heard his plea? "My sheep know me, and they hear my voice. If another calls to them they won't follow, but I give them free choice. Do you understand the saying of how the devil wants to sift you as wheat? It means to take all the good out of you and cast you out under men's feet. Ye are the salt of this world, yes; you are the spice in many people's day. If someone does you wrong, don't worry, for him God will repay. Stop working so hard for nothing, seek me and I will give you rest. See, you have been tried by fire, and my beloved you have passed the test."

TKO

What would Ernest do, take a TKO or get back into the fight?
Stand up and shine for God and for everything that's right.
Get back all that he lost to the lifestyle that he once lived
Not letting anything get in his way, believing God and
remembering To pray.
What would Ernest do, let the devil drive his '55 or drive
it himself? See, Ernest knows the way, the truth, the life,
so what else does Ernest need? Only to fasten his seat belt.
Look out, world, here comes me trying to make up laps
for a race that I haven't been in for a long time.
This is my victory lap without coke & wine.

Medusa

I can't help but feel the pain that has come across our land. The feeling that reaches and touches the soul of every woman and man. Medusa, with the power to turn one into stone if you were to look into her eyes, as America looks on, I can feel that my nation's spirit has cried. Some of our hearts has seen Medusa because they have already turned to stone, thinking only about oneself. Has all the feeling of compassion gone? I know that Medusa is not real, and that she comes from Greek fairy tales. Now if she's not alive in America today, well, brother, I can't tell. I have seen my fellow American's hearts, and they wear them on their sleeves. They forgot the little simple things and saying "thank you very much" and "please." When was the last time you showed love and did something about our problem, knowing that it's so easy to sit back and hope that someone else solve them? If you hear these words and your heart can feel America's pain, just stop and look Medusa straight in her eye because her modern day name is Cocaine. A preacher standing in the pulpit where he has forgotten how to preach. A man, woman, boy, or girl whose life is just out of reach. The queen of Sheba, she was fine until she forgot about her looks. My son in junior high used to bring home straight A's, but lately, he forgets about his books. Just look at Mike Tyson, man, has he forgotten how to box. The lady with the bald head get this, her name is Goldilocks. The man who live under the bridge on the interstate had a home and wife, but old snakehead touched him, and he forgot about his family life. The rich man from Wall Street, he's not rich anymore. The good lady down the street, I hate to tell you, but she is nothing but a whore. Please hear these words I have spoken and listen to them well. If not, Medusa will ride our nation head on straight to hell.

Day by Day

One day a bum begging, the next day, I am eating with the king.
One day can't even hold a note, the next day, with the angel I sing.
One day on the bottom, the next day on the top
One day just a seed, the next day the cream of the crop.

Hocus Pocus

Do I pray to A GOD that sits high and looks low,
OR my prays trapped here between the ceiling and the floor?
Bad things happen to good people, Good people doing
bad things.
Going to church on Sunday pray to God now you are changed
Abracadabra hocus pocus I just got out of another fix.
Is that the way you think about God, as an old man doing tricks?
Brother, you are wrong, I am right, you don't understand.
I've been going to church for forty years, I am a Christian man.

Roger Will-Co

Well, here I am at the VA; this is where I'll make my stand
And quit doing drugs at the age of fifty-five, get on my feet
and be a man. All is lost and without hope, I hope that I can comply.
Because if I keep going the way I am going, I will surely DIE.

Boom Boom Damn It Boom

I have spoken lies into the wind, both in the light where darkness dwells. Knowing that I'm an hour older by the sounding of the steeple bells. Boom, it's one o'clock (boom boom it's two), what have I done with my life? Boom, boom, it's four o'clock, I forgot I had a wife, boom, five hours has come and gone. Boom, boom, boom, I wish those bells would leave me alone. Three more booms and the witching hour comes, what do I care or what do I supposed to do? Midnight or high noon, the bell tolls for me and you.

Noda

Black ain't black anymore, the white grow up to be yippies
We hang out in Noda all day, eating pizza and alligator.
Everyone own a condo, rides a bike, our dogs are in the kennel
down the road. Oh, yes, the grill on the deck and new castle in
the refrigerator.

Peace of Mind

The addicted mind is one of a kind. It can only think one way,
But keep trying to change for the better each and every day,
Now the same stuff will keep happening, it starts early
in the morning. Night falls but don't break; day breaks
without warning,
Now, what, my friend, it's up to you, so what the hell are
you going to do, ride the same horse? You are in the same race.
I know you can make it, I can see it in your face, So get some
help from God, he will give you what you need, peace of
mind, you had better get on the hurry-up. We are running out of time.

My Boat

One of these days, when I wake up, this nightmare will be over and my ship will have come in. Slick back my hair and call me Frankie, this time I know I will win.

God and Mom

Bless the Lord always because he saved us from the pit of hell. He saved us from our self-destructive minds, dead and stinking can't you even smell? Everyone will give up on you—your friends, sister, and brother—but not God and Mom. The full-breasted one with the mighty arm.

Short Trip

In your life what made you flip? Was it acid or did you take a bad trip? Regress back to childhood now, tell me, do you remember? Did you get what you wanted that day on the twenty-fifth of December? Did you have your parent's love to show you the way, or did you get locked up in a room and could not go outside to play? Move forward now in school, did they call you a nerd, geek, or wussy? Just because you are sixteen years old and never even saw a pussy. Or was it after that when you said piss on it and went and joined the service? You come back from the war and everybody ask you, "Homeboy, why are you so nervous? Don't you know you need a job? How are your bills going to get paid?" But you just can't get rid of that memory when your platoon, they got hit by a rocket-propelled grenade. I bet you remember the smell of rice patties, them sons of a bitches did stink. Say, "Brother, what's that in that little bag you are holding? How about giving me a drink. I know that you can make it, man, don't go out like no punk." I guess it's all right sometimes to set back and get pissy drunk.

The Sky

Good-by till morrow, hope to see you in the sky
Good-by till morrow, the only way I don't see you is if I die.

Live Green

Life is green, my life is brown.
Nothing makes any sense, I'm just hanging around
Plants give life the simple way, we make life as we kneel down
and pray. As you talk to God the one that you should love.
Listen for his voice like a whisper soft as a dove.
He always speaks to us, always in a gentle way
That is why I listen and speak to my God every single day.

Just Do It

I want to go to heaven, but I don't want to die.
I want to quit doing drugs, but I don't want to try.

Art

A monkey grabs a paint brush, an elephant grabs one, too. It sold for $100,000, not to me how about you? To understand art is to understand the human mind. So if you want some monkey art, well, here's some wavy lines. Is it hip to wear things you know don't look good? Or do you wear some garment because society said you should? As the king walked through his kingdom one day, I spoke up and said, "He has nothing on but his crown." He thought of how naked he was, and now he's wearing his crown and a reddened frown. The king should have been his own man and believed his own eyes. People want you to look like a fool, and they will tell you lies. The cool you saved from being embarrassed will be yours, so please be smart. Consider the king and his nakedness the next time you buy any art.

My Life

I don't like the way I am living my life, I can't stop doing wrong. I am weak. I want to do the right thing. God says you can have just what you speak. Free will is hard for me, after living in this world of sin. To make it to the finish line, only to finish this race that I am in. To kill the person that I am and to start all over from the start. All I want from God is for him to touch my stoney heart. I can't curse the day that I was born. It was a day like all the others. Sometimes I think about cursing everyone in this world, including my father and mother. I can't change me, I need help from God. I need a miracle to save my soul. As I listen on the wind, I hear a bell and wonder for whom does it tolls.

Give a Child a Chance

God has given us all the right to the tree of life, I don't have any pity if a man lives under a bridge. That is of his own accord; seems like he gave up on life, that's probably what he did. But for a child to be without the bare essentials of life, not to mention a place to lay their head at night, he or she has gotten off to a bad start. Just think of all the memories they have to endure for the rest of their life. Scars that will never heal or keep them from dying, as they search for that mythical creator called love. They need this love that they can see now, not a dream that people tell them of. I have said enough, I don't won't to bore you, just enjoy the night and keep up the good work, we are not in this alone. Before it's over, hopefully, every child that is without a house will one day have a HOME.

Help Yourself

Why do you think that the world owes you something just be-
cause you are black? This is a America, my brothers and sisters,
if you don't have what you want there is something that you lack.
You can walk around and pick up beer cans all day, I see a lot of
people do. But you have a lot of pride, and you don't want your
friends to see you. I tell you what, ask your friends to help you
until you get back on your feet. They won't give you a plate of
beans, now that you're down they want to see you sleep on the
street. Believe me, homeboy, once bitten twice shy, do learn from
my mistakes please. Because the only thing this world owes you
is a "bless you" after you sneeze.

Armageddon

Gunshots ring through the night, I wonder who got blasted this time. Was it someone in my family, your brother, sister, or maybe one of mine? This life has gotten everyone up in arms; the night holds secrets no man can know. Hurry, daylight, come quickly, so I can unlock my front door; blood run freely in the street as deep as to the horses' bridle. It's the blood of our nation, my brother, black, white, rich or poor, it really don't matter. Jails don't help the convicts, it only makes them mean and worse. The young people out in the streets seem like for blood they thirst. It will stop one of these days, God said so, Armageddon is man's fate. If God don't shorten the days, it will be all over, but he will for the elect's sake.

Hind Sight

The other side of reality deep six arms folded across your chest. Are you grateful to be dead, no more games of life, did you do your best? If we could see with dead men's eyes, what would be the story that we would tell. Behind those black and lifeless eyes, we look up in heaven or across the Gulf in Hell. Would there be tears of joy or tears of fear? Only the dead man knows, but he won't speak. Tell me, in this life, what did you do, and, brother, whom did you seek? Did you search for everlasting life? If not, may God have mercy on your undying soul. Next time you hear the church bell ring, you will answer the question: For whom the bell tolls? It tolls for thee, telling you to change your ways because time is running out. One of these days, we will see what the dead man sees very clear without doubt.

The Year 2000

Nineteen ninety-nine is right around the bend, who knows what the new millennium will bring? All the things on Star Trek and the Jetsons nowadays don't mean a thing. Designer drugs are here to stay; they help you to leave your problem behind. You don't fry your ham and eggs anymore; you take a placebo and fry your mind. Who is big brother, is he tracking, I mean, watching you? He does them both and does it with microchips. If someone would have told me this in the '70s I would have said, "Man, are you on acid or having a bad trip?" But now I see my money, my MasterCard's, and my life on a screen on the Internet. Go to the Cherokee reservation if you want to gamble, but on life don't take any bets.

Tryon Hills Mom

I bet you know my mama if you live in Tryon Hills. Everybody loves her because of the way she makes them feel. Some mothers don't talk to you, they act like they don't have the time. You must be talking about someone else's mama; I know you are not talking about mine. If you are hungry and need a bite to eat or a dollar to catch the bus, you know that you can get it from my mom, because she treats you like one of us. All my friends love my mom, and when they see me, they ask how my mom is doing—well, I hope. I say, "Yes, fine, thank you." She is still praying for all her boys and girls who are still out there doing dope. Mama has been praying for a long time, and I see that it is doing some good. All you have to do is look at the change around the neighborhood. Every mom ought to pray to God and treat the kids of Tryon Hills like their own. Then maybe you will feel safe to go for a walk at night alone.

The Contest

Hey, Mister Artist, could you please rush? We need to have church here in the Sistine Chapel, and Mister William Tell could you go ahead and shoot? Don't worry about your son. See, I bought the apple. I have not seen a masterpiece on canvas or scroll from Shakespeare to Vincent Van Gogh. That didn't take some time and effort, and now you give us twenty lines or less. Where is the logic in this? I sure don't know. So this contest is some kind of scam to milk people with talent out of a little money. You probably don't even read two-thirds of them. I guess that you think that it's kind of funny. You might send the little free gift but, sir, you asked for our best. Well, I have got to bring this letter to a close, you know I am coming up on twenty lines or less.

All You Do Is Stop

Well, I believe I am the biggest fool of them all. I lost everything I had, and I still play around with that ball. Seems like I am possessed by that devil known as crack. I can see it coming, I know that he is on the attack. I don't know how to stop unless stop is all you do. Maybe I will try that, I don't want to lose my wife, too.

Mother

…sometimes you look right through me and see all the wrong that I've done, but sometimes love won't let you, because I'm your loving son.

To hurt someone you love is a hurt that's like no other, especially when the one I hurt was you, my precious Mother.

They say only God can make a tree. I look at them and believe it, but a mother's love is stronger than any. Now I open my heart and receive it.

You are like a mighty fortress standing by me if I'm right or wrong. I remember as a little boy I was sick, and you sang my favorite song.

I look back on life with pure amazement, and often I sit and wonder not knowing but now seeing a love that no one can tear asunder.

If I could, for you, each day I would ring the Sistine Chapel's bells, because little boys are made of three things. The last one is puppy dogs' tails.

I just had to say that, Mother, I love to see you smile.
The bells I would truly ring to be heard for miles and miles.

Sometimes mothers don't hear this enough. Mom, you are overdue. These snakes and snails and puppy dogs' tails really do love you.

Time

I'll give my body time to heal, and give mine time
to feel. All the emotion that comes my way. The answer to
the question that I must say.
To fly to the top as the hawk has done
To have my portion under the sun.

Ride-Write On

You fix a flat, I write another line. One job is yours
one job is mine, you help people get back on the road,
I help a classroom to understand stuff that they never know.
To see things in a different light, That is why I chose the
PEN, That is why I write. Another thing is I don't get down
and dirty, and one more is that I don't have to get started too
early. I try to use my top instead of my bottom.
Very few know how to use them if they got' em.
To get to the point that they need to be, now you will
be hindered on every side. Brother, just don't give up; it can
be done. Walk instead of ride, take time to smell the rose,
that is why when I finish people say, "See, I know it." Not
like the hog with the big head, and he don't know everything.
Sometimes we have to turn the page and come in out of the rain.

Round #2

What can I do? Probably nothing. To stop meeting her in
my sleep, the things that we do I can't share I must keep.
I have told her in the past my heart feeling she just
laughed…but then there's the way she looks at me, is it
my heart, or just gas?
This has been going on seems like forever. And I don't want
it to stop. No woman on earth has ever had my mind so tied
up in a knot. Is this a test from GOD to see if I will do right?
I've been doing good so far, hiding my emotions and winning
this fight.

Your Turn at Bat

Another responsibility, not like feeding the cat or walking the dog. Any dickhead can do that. Now try taking care of a woman. Now that's stepping up to bat.

No Limit

The sky is the limit? Well, maybe for some
The eagle flies through the heavens; his heart reaching for the sun.
It rises and sits from the east to the west.
Each day, as we start, we will be put to the test.
Just enough for one day. One of them at a time
So is the sky the limit? No, not for me and my mind.

The Fat Sung

Who cares when the fat lady sings; there's not a thing that you can do. So, if you are doing wrong, keep on doing what you do.
Right is good to do, and if wishes only come true once a year, my only wish would be that my righteousness would come and stay here.

The Graveyard Shift

The witching hour strikes, and things start to come alive. I should be at home in bed; that's why in the morning I have red eyes. I can't wait to get off work now; that's around 4:30. I do a little bit of work around the house; see, I don't want to get started too early. As soon as the sun goes down, the freaks start to move about. Most of the time, you can spot their cars because they have a headlight or window knocked out. How much money am I going to spend tonight? I don't know or even care. Stores that stay open late, I tell you what they better beware. If I run out of money, I'll start to steal anything to make a few bucks. I'll take anything, lying around in your yard, so you better lock your shit up. Chainsaws, lawnmowers, weed eaters, bicycles, tricycles, too. Anything is fair game, my brother, I'm not taking from me—I'm taking from you. Frankenstein, werewolves, and vampires, and all kinds of monsters used to keep me up at night. But crack addicts are scarier than any I know—I give myself a fright. We walk around like zombies, we are the living dead. To steal from your mother and father you have got to be out of your head. Well, I am trying to quit the graveyard shift and get a good nine to five, and let the zombies have all that late night activity and all the other jive. But things that go creep and bump in the night—don't look out your window, because you might see. If your gas grill or your dog is gone, that creeper might be me.

Grandma

To share the wisdom of old, she was the family tree. Let me sit down with you awhile, let me cut off the radio and TV. A lot of the old folks are dead, but Grandma still remembers them as plain as yesterday in her head. "Grandpa left me first," she says, "and then a son and a daughter," then she scratches her head and says to me, "Well, maybe not in that order. I am glad that you want to sit a spell, seems like no one ever wants to sit and talk." Then I say, "I tell you what, Grandma, get your snuff and let's go for a walk." As we start out of the door, I put her sweater over her shoulders. I say, "Grandma, we have done this many times before." She says, "Yes, but now I get much colder. I don't move as fast as I used to; look at the sky, we are going to get some rain." "How do you know that, Grandma?" She tell me, "God makes it very plain." "But the weather man said it would be sunny all week, and there's not a cloud in the sky." Grandma just shrugs her shoulder, I know she has cataracts in her eyes. She points to the tree that Grandpa planted, it's still standing straight and tall. I see the old bicycle rim rusted there, where I used to play basketball. Back there is where the smokehouse stood, and over there was the pigpen. Then I heard her say to herself, "I guess I will never see that kind of stuff again." As the day goes by, we laugh and cry as this day is almost gone. Then she gets a little more snuff and we head towards the east and home. "Grandma, I enjoyed this evening." Then suddenly, I see a flash of lightning across the sky. I say, "It's going to rain, Grandma." She says, "God will never tell me a lie."

My Girl

Hey, girl, what are you doing with all your mama's makeup on? Oh! you scared me, Daddy, I did not know that you were home. Don't I look cute all dressed up, and am I your favorite girl?" "You look just like your mother you are the most precious thing in my world." "I made you some mud pies today, Daddy, I made them all by myself. Mama wouldn't let me make them in the house, but I put you one under the shelf. Daddy, tell me what I am made of again, I'll try to remember tonight." "You are made of roses and baby bunny rabbits, my dear, and summer butterflies in flight. The softness of one snowflake, the sweetness of a honey dew, the rays of the morning sun as it says good morning to you." "Daddy, do you like this lipstick, mama's hat, and matching pearls? When I grow up, Daddy, will mom and I still be your favorite girls?" "Sweetheart, if ever there comes a time in your life and you think that my love for you has changed, just look up at the rainbow in the sky after it rains."

The Last Will Be First

They say that only the good die young. Well, that's the way that it seems. Has my death been in vain? Once a year, you remember me or my speech. I have a dream. Don't let my dream become a nightmare. What has happened in the black community? The way that it looks from where I sit since I left there is very little unity. As far as jobs and education goes, you don't want to work, and in your son's backpack, he carries a gun. What about all the freedom I fought for? You are losing all the victories that I won. All across America the progress of black people seems to be regressing instead of proceeding. You kill me all over again in Memphis. In my grave my heart is still bleeding. If you can't only remember me once a year, you will be destined to repeat the past. Can't you remember and still hear my words ringing in your ear? Thank God Almighty, we are free at last.

Clean-up on One

Man, I never thought life would do me like this.
I am pushing a shopping cart, and I am not shopping.
I've being doing this for years now, and I don't see any stopping.
Doing what I have to do to get drugs, I keep them on my
mind. Don't have any food on my table, but I got half on
the next bottle of wine.
My world is out of whack, I just simply let my guard down.
Will someone please throw me a lifeline? Seems like I am lost
at sea, and I am about to drown.

The United States: Police of the World

Stop. You can't do that; you don't have the right. We're the United States, and we say big boys don't fight. If you do, we'll come get you, and we'll restore law and order. So piss on you, France, and any other country that won't let us cross borders. We have big jets and tankers that can outfly Russian MIGs. And our B-1 Stealth bombers can drop bombs on any grid. Laser guided missile that we shoot from our ships' decks. Just ask Saddam and Khadafi, we left their homelands in wrecks. The big two wars and Korea, we add them to our list. The Bay of Pigs and Vietnam was just a hit and miss. Now we know how to do things, so watch out you pinko-commie bastard, or we'll nuke you and those other pigs and sit back and laugh after. Now you know that we don't want to fight, we would rather feed the hungry of the world, dude. Just don't mind that man on the corner that says, "I have a family and will work for food. This is the land of much a plenty, and we can't even take care of ourselves." People in other parts of the world are getting fat while I am tightening my belt. They don't appreciate our help; they are like dogs that bit the hand that give them bread. U.N. peacekeeper soldier marine left home wanting to help. Now some are dead. I love my brothers, but like the old saying goes "Kill them all and let God sort them out." Their like that itsy-bitsy spider that went up that water spout. As soon as the sun comes out and all is well and good, the warlords are back on the front to take all their much-needed food. So let the warlord have them come home, and we'll police ourselves. Poor Rodney King got stopped, and he wasn't wearing his seatbelt. But just like poor Rodney says, "Can't we all just get along." Police the world, I don't think so, Mr. President. Please bring our BOYS HOME.